Inspiring Stories for Amazing Boys Who Believe in Themselves

21 Short Stories About Courage, Self-Confidence, Overcoming Fear & Empowering Young Minds in Just 5 Minutes a Day

By

Sati Siroda

Book Ecke

Inspiring Stories for Amazing Boys Who Believe in Themselves

21 Short Stories About Courage, Self-Confidence, Overcoming Fear & Empowering Young Minds in Just 5 Minutes a Day

By

Sati Siroda

Published by Book Ecke
15A, 4th Floor, City Vista, Tower A,
Suite No.1140, Fountain Road, Kharadi, Pune - 411014
Website: www.bookecke.com

ISBN

eBook: 978-81-985337-9-1

Paperback: 978-81-985337-2-2

Hardback: 978-81-985337-7-7

First edition [2025]

Visit www.bookecke.com for any further information.

To every incredible boy who dares to believe in himself, to every young heart that rises after a fall, and to every dreamer who sees endless possibilities within—this book is for you. May you always find the strength to stand tall, the courage to face your fears, and the confidence to shine as brightly as the stars. The world is yours to explore, to create, and to conquer. Keep believing, keep growing, and never stop being amazing.

... and Thank You, Charlie Piper!

BOOKS BY SATI SIRODA

Mind the Quote

Coffee Tales: Short Stories of Wisdom

Earnest Poetica: Ink Expressions of the Ineffable Heart

Gratitude Journal: Reflect, Appreciate, Transform in 60 Days

Inspiring Stories for Amazing Girls Who Believe in Themselves

Table of Contents

Your Free Gift

Hi there, Rockstar! 🌟

I have a special surprise just for you—not one, but **TWO** incredible e-books to make your day even brighter! These free gifts are packed with fun, creativity, and inspiration:

1. **Supercars Coloring Book with Fun Facts**
    - Superb illustrations of supercars and fascinating facts to enjoy.
2. **Dare to Dream: 10 Inspiring Stories for Brave Kids**
    - Ten powerful tales filled with adventure, life lessons, and affirmations.

Just ask your awesome grown-up to scan the QR code to grab your free e-books!

Scan Me

Introduction

Welcome, Future Trailblazer!

Did you know

Every great adventure begins with a challenge. Every hero, every inventor, every champion you look up to once faced moments of doubt. They weren't always fearless. They didn't always know what they were doing. But here's what set them apart—they didn't let uncertainty hold them back. They kept going, took chances, and discovered just how strong they truly were.

That's exactly what this book is about.

Welcome to *Inspiring Stories for Boys Who Believe in Themselves*—a collection of short, powerful stories designed to show you that you are capable of more than you think. Think of it as your playbook for confidence and courage, filled with quick, engaging stories to help you tackle life's challenges. And the best part? Each story takes just five minutes to read!

What This Book is All About

Have you ever wanted to try something new but felt nervous? Ever wondered if you were good enough? Ever failed at something and thought about giving up? Here's the truth—everyone experiences those feelings, even the most successful people in the world.

But here's the difference: those who succeed don't let fear win. They learn, they adapt, and they keep moving forward. This book will show you how to do the same.

Inside, you'll meet boys who face real struggles—standing up for themselves, chasing big dreams, pushing through failures. Through their stories, you'll learn how to turn obstacles into stepping stones and doubts into confidence.

Why You'll Love It

1. Exciting, action-packed stories—no boring lessons, just engaging adventures.
2. Big ideas, short reads—perfect for a quick break that makes a lasting impact.
3. Lessons you can actually use—because confidence and courage aren't just words; they're skills you can build.
4. Challenges and affirmations—each story has activities to help you apply what you've learned.
5. It's all about YOU—becoming the strongest, smartest, and most confident version of yourself.

What Made Me Write This Book (And Why It's Meant for You)

When I was your age, I had my fair share of doubts. I questioned whether I was good enough, whether I could handle tough situations, whether I had what it takes to succeed. But then I discovered something that changed everything—stories have the power to shift the way we see ourselves and the world.

Stories made me realize that bravery isn't about never being scared—it's about moving forward even when you are. They showed me that failure isn't the end—it's the beginning of something better. And most of all, they reminded me that the only limits in life are the ones we accept.

That's why I wrote this book. Not just to entertain you but to show you what's possible when you start believing in yourself. Because the truth is—you are already capable of more than you know.

Ready to Begin?

Find a comfortable spot, settle in, and dive into the first story. Your adventure starts NOW!

With love,

Sati

Part 1: The Courage to Take the First Step

Hey, Trailblazer!

Did you know that astronauts spend *years* training, preparing, and facing their fears before they fly into space? But no rocket ever launched without *the very* first step—someone daring to say, *"I'm ready to try!"*

Starting something new can feel overwhelming. Whether it's joining a new club, learning a new skill, or speaking up in class, that first step takes courage. But every hero's journey begins the same way—by moving forward, even when it feels scary.

In this section, you'll meet boys just like you who faced their fears and took that first step. And guess what? *You* can, too. So, what's your first step going to be? Let's get started!

Chapter 1: Zane's Brave Answer

Zane sat at his desk, staring at the question written on the whiteboard. His heart pounded like a drum. He knew the answer. He was sure of it. But what if he was wrong? What if everyone laughed? The last time he spoke up, someone giggled when he stumbled over his words. Ever since then, Zane had decided it was safer to stay quiet.

"Who can tell me what the main idea of this paragraph is?" Ms. Carter asked, scanning the classroom.

Zane felt his fingers twitch. He knew the answer. He could feel the words forming in his head. He swallowed hard, his eyes flickering toward the clock. Maybe if he waited long enough, someone else would answer, and he wouldn't have to.

But no one did. The classroom remained silent.

Zane clenched his fists under his desk. His teacher always told them that every answer—right or wrong—was a step toward learning. He thought about his mom's constant reminder, "Bravery isn't about not being scared; it's about doing something even when you are."

Slowly, Zane raised his hand.

Ms. Carter's face lit up. "Yes, Zane?"

His voice wavered as he said, "I think the main idea is about how teamwork makes big challenges easier."

The class was silent for a second. Then, Ms. Carter nodded. "That's an excellent answer! And can you tell us why you think that?"

Zane hesitated. Then, something incredible happened. His fear started to shrink. He took a deep breath and explained his reasoning. When he finished, Ms. Carter smiled.

"Very well explained, Zane! That's exactly right."

Instead of laughing, a few classmates murmured, "Yeah, that makes sense," and "I was thinking that too."

Zane sat back in his chair. His heart was still racing, but this time, it wasn't fear—it was excitement. He had spoken up. And nothing terrible had happened. In fact, it felt... amazing.

What Zane Learned

Zane learned that speaking up can lead to great things, even when it feels scary. His voice mattered, and even if he made a mistake, it was part of learning. Courage isn't about never being afraid—it's about doing the hard thing anyway.

Affirmation for Speaking Up

Write this affirmation in your notebook and repeat it before class or any time you need confidence:

"My thoughts and ideas are important. I am brave enough to share them."

Try This

- Think of a place or activity you've avoided because it seemed too scary or difficult. Can you take one small step toward it?
- Create a "Confidence Journal" where you write about moments when you spoke up or tried something new. To make it more fun, add drawings or stickers.
- Plan a "Courage Challenge"! Choose one small challenge, like trying a new food or talking to someone new, and treat it like an adventure. Reflect on how you felt before and after—you may be surprised by your own bravery!

Zane's story reminds us that courage grows every time we take a small step forward. What will you speak up about next?

Chapter 2: Richard's Big Game

Richard's heart pounded as he stepped onto the court. The final game of the season was here, and the basketball court was packed with cheering fans. His team had trained hard for this, and tonight, they were ready to prove themselves. But Richard couldn't shake the nervous energy coursing through him. What if they lost? What if he missed the final shot?

The game began with intensity. The opposing team was fast, their defense strong. Richard dribbled past a defender and passed the ball to his teammate, who took the shot—missed. The other team rebounded and scored, taking an early lead. The pressure was on.

By halftime, Richard's team was down by ten points. The locker room was silent, the weight of the game hanging over them. Coach Morales clapped his hands together. "Alright, team. We've trained for this. We know how to push through. It's not about winning—it's about playing the best game we can."

Richard met his teammates' eyes. They weren't giving up. They were ready to fight for every point.

The second half started with renewed energy. Richard pushed himself harder, weaving through defenders and making quick passes. His teammates responded, their confidence growing with each successful play. The score tightened, and with two minutes left on the clock, they were only two points behind.

Then it happened. Richard saw his opening, took the shot—and missed. The other team grabbed the ball, raced down the court, and scored. The final buzzer rang. They had lost.

Richard felt the disappointment hit him like a wave. He had given everything, and it still hadn't been enough. But as he looked around at his teammates, he saw something else: *pride.* They had played their hearts out. And that mattered more than the final score.

Instead of dwelling on the loss, Richard and his team doubled down. Every afternoon, they practiced harder, refining their skills and pushing each other to improve. They didn't just want to win—they wanted to be the best team they could be.

When the next season rolled around, Richard felt stronger. Their first game was against the same team they had lost to. This time, it was different. His team played with confidence, matching their opponents point for point. The final seconds ticked down, and the score was tied. Richard took the last shot—and missed. But so did the other team.

The game ended in a tie, and instead of feeling disappointed, Richard felt something new: *satisfaction.* It had been an incredible game, full of energy, teamwork, and growth. He had played his best, and that was enough.

What Richard Learned

Richard learned that success isn't just about winning—it's about effort, growth, and resilience. Hard work and perseverance made him a stronger player, and even when victory wasn't his, the journey was still worth it.

Affirmation for Determination

Write this affirmation in your notebook and repeat it whenever you need motivation:

"Every step I take makes me stronger. I learn, I grow, and I never give up."

Try This

- Think of a time when you felt discouraged. Write about how you handled it and what you learned from the experience.
- Set a new goal in something you love, whether it's sports, music, or another skill. Track your progress and celebrate your improvement, not just the outcome.
- Create a "Resilience Journal" where you write about challenges and how you pushed through them. Reflecting on your growth can inspire you in future challenges.

Richard's story reminds us that the journey matters just as much as the destination. What challenge will you face next?

Chapter 3: Jeffrey's Guitar Journey

Jeffrey had always admired great guitarists. He would sit in the audience, mesmerized by the way they played with such confidence and ease. He wished he could do the same, but doubt crept in every time he picked up his guitar. Could he ever be that good?

One day, he decided to try. He started practicing daily, even if it was just for a few minutes. At first, his fingers stumbled over the strings, and the melodies sounded rough. But he didn't give up. He celebrated small victories—playing a song without mistakes, learning a new chord, or performing in front of his family. As his confidence grew, he sought out mentors who could guide him. His music teacher encouraged him, and his friends cheered him on. With their support, he signed up for a school music competition.

The weeks before the competition were filled with practice. Jeffrey played until his fingers ached, refining every note. He visualized himself standing on stage, feeling confident, and performing his best. Some days were frustrating—he would mess up, forget chords, and feel like giving up. But each time, he reminded himself that courage was about pushing through challenges.

When the day of the competition arrived, Jeffrey's hands shook as he stepped onto the stage. The crowd was silent as he positioned his fingers on the strings. His heart pounded. What if he failed? What if everyone laughed at him?

Taking a deep breath, Jeffrey closed his eyes for a second. He remembered all his practice and small victories that had led him here. Then, he began to play.

The first few notes filled the auditorium, clear and strong. As he played, his nerves faded away. His fingers danced across the strings, and he lost himself in the music. When he hit the final note, the room erupted into applause. Jeffrey couldn't believe it—he had done it!

Later that evening, the results were announced. Jeffrey had won first place! He could hardly believe it. The boy who once doubted himself had just won a music competition. But more than the trophy, Jeffrey had gained something even more valuable—confidence in his abilities.

What Jeffrey Learned

Jeffrey learned that courage isn't about being fearless; it's about taking small steps, building confidence, and believing in yourself. The more he practiced stepping outside his comfort zone, the stronger his confidence grew.

Affirmation for Bravery

Write this affirmation in your notebook and repeat it before taking on a challenge:

"I trust my abilities, and I embrace challenges as opportunities to grow."

Try This

- Think of something you've always wanted to try but felt nervous about. Set a small goal to take the first step.
- Keep a journal of your progress. Write down small victories, even if they seem tiny—they add up!
- Visualize yourself succeeding. Close your eyes and imagine yourself doing the thing that scares you with confidence and skill.

Jeffrey's story reminds us that we can achieve great things with perseverance and courage. What will you take the first step toward today?

Part 2: Unlocking the Confidence Code

Hey, Go-Getter!

Confidence isn't about always winning or being the best. It's about *believing* in yourself, even when things don't go perfectly. Think about athletes before a big game or musicians before a concert. They don't always know what will happen, but they trust in their training, their skills, and their ability to keep going.

But here's the thing—confidence isn't something you're just born with. It's like a muscle that grows stronger whenever you try, learn, and keep pushing forward.

In this section, you'll meet boys who discovered the secret to confidence: taking small steps, learning from mistakes, and never giving up. By the end, you'll have your own *Confidence Code* to unlock new possibilities. Ready to believe in yourself? Let's go!

Chapter 4: William's Path to Responsibility

William loved playing with his toys. His room was filled with action figures, race cars, and building blocks. But there was one problem—he never cleaned up after himself. His toys were scattered across the floor, his books were piled up on his desk, and his clothes lay unfolded on his bed. His dad often reminded him to clean up, but William would always say, "I'll do it later."

One day, his dad walked into his room and sighed. "William, you need to start taking responsibility for your space. You can't keep living in this mess."

William shrugged. "It's just toys, Dad. I know where everything is."

His dad sat on the bed. "William, being responsible isn't just about knowing where things are. It's about taking care of them and creating a space where you can focus and grow. A messy space can make it hard to think clearly."

William still didn't understand why it was such a big deal. But that evening, when he tripped over his building blocks and knocked over a cup of water onto his favorite comic book, he realized maybe his dad was right.

Determined to change, William decided to take small steps. The next morning, he made his bed for the first time without being asked. At first, it felt strange, but it also made his room look nicer. Then, he picked up his toys before going to bed. It took only a few minutes, but it felt good waking up to a clean room.

William began noticing something: keeping his room organized made him feel more in control. He didn't lose his favorite toys anymore and had space to do his homework without pushing things aside. Cleaning up didn't feel like a chore anymore; it felt like an accomplishment.

Sometimes, there were days when William didn't feel like cleaning, but he reminded himself why it was important. He wrote a list of reasons and taped it to his door:

- A clean room helps me focus.
- I won't lose my toys.
- I feel proud when my space is neat.

His dad noticed his efforts. "I'm proud of you, William. You're taking responsibility, and that's a big part of growing up."

One weekend, his dad surprised him with a new shelf for his toys. "This is for all your hard work," he said. William smiled as he organized his action figures on the shelf. For the first time, he understood what his dad meant about responsibility.

What William Learned

William learned that responsibility isn't about doing chores—it's about taking pride in your space and actions. Small, consistent steps build confidence, and taking ownership of his room made him feel capable and strong.

Affirmation for Responsibility

Write this affirmation in your notebook and repeat it whenever you need motivation:

"I take responsibility for my space and actions. I understand that small steps lead to big achievements."

Try This

- Pick one small habit to improve, like making your bed or organizing your desk, and stick to it every day for a week.
- Set a daily reminder to tidy up one small area of your space, like your desk or a shelf, and see how it improves your focus and mood.
- Find a responsibility buddy—someone who also wants to build good habits. Keep each other accountable and celebrate progress together.

William's story shows us that responsibility and inner confidence grow through small actions. What will you take charge of today?

Chapter 5: Benjamin's Path to Courage

Benjamin sat in his math class, staring at the numbers on the board. No matter how hard he tried, the equations never made sense. His classmates seemed to understand, quickly scribbling answers in their notebooks, but Benjamin felt lost. He didn't want to ask for help—what if they thought he wasn't smart enough? Every day, he struggled with homework and dreaded math class. One evening, his older sister noticed his frustration. "Why don't you ask for help?" she asked gently.

Benjamin sighed. "I don't want people to think I can't do it on my own."

His sister smiled. "Asking for help doesn't mean you're weak. It means you're strong enough to learn."

Benjamin thought about it all night. The next day, he raised his hand in class and asked a question. His teacher explained patiently, and for the first time, the numbers started making sense. That day, Benjamin realized that courage isn't about knowing everything—it's about being willing to learn.

Determined to improve, Benjamin set small goals. He asked his teacher for extra help after school, practiced math problems for just ten minutes a day, and celebrated every small success—like solving a tough problem correctly. Each step made him feel more confident.

As weeks passed, Benjamin noticed a change. Math wasn't as scary anymore. He still struggled sometimes, but instead of feeling ashamed, he reminded himself that learning took time. He even helped a friend struggling with math problems, realizing that asking for help had made him stronger.

One day, his teacher stood in front of the class with a knowing smile. "Alright, class, today is the day of your math quiz!"

Benjamin's stomach did a little flip. A test? Already? But then, he remembered all the hard work he had put in—the extra practice, the questions he had bravely asked, the persistence he had shown. He took a deep breath and reminded himself, *I can do this!*

With a determined nod, he picked up his pencil and got to work. He took his time, recalling the steps his teacher had explained and the tricks he had learned. For the first time, he didn't feel lost in a sea of numbers—he felt focused, ready, and in control.

When the results came back, he could hardly believe his eyes. A big, bold *A* was written at the top of his paper! His heart soared.

His teacher beamed. "Fantastic work, Benjamin! You've worked hard for this, and it shows."

Benjamin grinned, his chest swelling with pride. He had done it! No because it was easy but because he dared to ask for help, keep trying, and believe in himself.

What Benjamin Learned

Benjamin learned that confidence is built through small actions. Admitting you need help isn't a weakness—it's a strength. With effort and persistence, challenges become opportunities to grow.

Affirmation for Growth

Write this affirmation in your notebook and repeat it when facing a challenge:
"I am always learning, I have the courage to ask for help, and every step I take makes me stronger."

Try This

- Think of something you struggle with and set a small, achievable goal to improve.
- Find a mentor, teacher, or friend who can guide you, and don't be afraid to ask for help.
- Keep a "Success Jar." Every time you achieve a small victory, write it down and place it in the jar. When you need encouragement, read about your past successes!

Benjamin's story reminds us that confidence comes from taking action, asking for help, and celebrating progress. What will you work on next?

Part 3: Fearless: Learning to Face the Unknown

Hey, Brave One!

Everyone feels fear—it's completely normal. Even the greatest explorers and athletes have been scared at some point. But what makes them different? They *don't let fear stop them*. Instead, they take a deep breath, step forward, and do what they thought they couldn't do.

Fear isn't a wall; it's a challenge. The more you face it, the smaller it becomes. Whether it's speaking up in class, standing up for what's right, or trying something new, every time you push through fear, you become stronger and more confident.

In this section, you'll read about boys who stood face-to-face with their fears—and didn't back down. By the end, you'll have the tools to do the same. Ready to take that step? Let's go!

Chapter 6: Larid's High Dive

Larid stood at the edge of the high diving board, his toes curled around the rough surface. Below him, the water sparkled under the bright sun. Kids splashed and laughed in the pool, diving off the board with ease. His heart pounded. He had climbed all the way up, but now, standing here, the height seemed impossible.

"Come on, Larid! You can do it!" his friend Noah cheered from below.

He wanted to jump—he really did. But his legs felt like jelly. His palms were sweaty, and a lump formed in his throat. What if he belly-flopped? What if he made a fool of himself?

His coach, Mark, stood at the poolside and called up, "Larid, remember what we practiced. Fear only wins if you let it. Take a deep breath and trust yourself."

Larid inhaled deeply and nodded. *I can do this.* He bent his knees and pushed off.

For a split second, he soared through the air. Then—

SPLASH!

Water exploded around him as he landed awkwardly, belly first. The sting made him wince, and for a moment, he hesitated under the water. But then, something surprising happened—he surfaced, gasping, and instead of hearing laughter, he heard cheers.

"You did it, Larid!" Noah shouted.

Mark grinned. "Great first dive! Now let's do it again."

But Larid wasn't convinced. His stomach still churned. His landing had been bad, and he still felt embarrassed. "Coach, what if I never get it right?"

Mark crouched beside the pool. "Every expert was once a beginner, Larid. The only way to get better is to keep going."

Larid swam to the ladder, climbed out, and looked back up at the board. The fear was still there, but it wasn't as big as before. He had faced it once. He could face it again.

With determination, he climbed up the board, took a deep breath, and leaped. Again. And again. Each time, he got better—his legs steadier, his dives smoother. His first few attempts were still awkward, and he flopped into the water more times than he could count. But every time he surfaced, Mark was there, nodding approvingly, and Noah clapped from the edge of the pool.

By the end of practice, Larid wasn't just diving—he was loving it. His final jump was smooth, controlled, and for the first time, he felt free. When he emerged from the water, he laughed. He had done it. Not perfectly, not instantly, but he had done it. And that was what mattered.

What Larid Learned

Larid learned that facing fear head-on makes it smaller. The first step is always the hardest, but with persistence, fear turns into confidence. Mistakes are just part of learning!

Affirmation for Facing Fear

Write this affirmation in your notebook and repeat it when you're feeling afraid:
"I am brave, and I grow stronger every time I face my fears."

Try This

- Think of something that scares you, like speaking in front of the class or trying a new sport. Take a small step toward it.
- Keep a "Fear Journal" and write about times you faced your fears. How did it feel before and after?
- Find a mentor, teacher, or coach who can guide you in overcoming a challenge. Having someone to encourage you makes a huge difference!

Larid's story reminds us that fear fades when we take action. What fear will you face today?

Chapter 7: Shawn's Search in the Dark

Shawn had never liked the dark. Shadows stretched too far, noises sounded louder, and every creak of the floor made his heart race. But tonight, he was facing his worst fear.

Oscar, his beloved golden retriever, was missing.

The wind howled outside as Shawn's mom and dad searched the backyard. His little sister, Emily, peeked under every table and bed. But Oscar was nowhere to be found.

"He must have gotten out," Dad said, pulling on his coat. "We should check the woods."

Shawn's stomach dropped. The woods? At night?

He peered through the window. The trees stood tall and black against the moonlight, their branches twisting like giant fingers. The path leading into the forest looked endless. Cold dread crawled up his spine.

"Let's wait until morning," he blurted out, his voice shaky.

Mom put a hand on his shoulder. "Oscar's out there, Shawn. He might be scared, too."

That thought sent a pang through Shawn's chest. Oscar had always been there for him—curling up beside him during thunderstorms, nudging his hand when he was sad. Shawn swallowed hard. *I have to do this.*

Dad handed him a flashlight. "We'll go together."

Shawn hesitated but then nodded. He zipped up his jacket and stepped onto the porch. The night was colder than he expected, the wind biting at his cheeks. His heart pounded as he took the first step toward the woods.

The trees swallowed them whole. The further they went, the darker it became. The flashlight beam bounced off the bark, but the shadows seemed to move. Every rustle in the leaves made Shawn's pulse jump.

He kept close to his dad, gripping the flashlight like a lifeline. "Oscar!" he called, his voice barely above a whisper.

A sudden snap of a branch made him freeze.

Dad turned. "Probably just the wind."

Shawn nodded, but his breath was shaky. *Or something worse?*

They walked deeper. Every step was a battle against the fear gripping his chest. His mind was filled with *what-ifs*—what if Oscar was hurt? What if something was lurking in the dark? What if they never found him?

"Shawn," Dad said gently, "I know this is scary. But fear isn't the enemy. It's just your brain trying to protect you. The key is knowing when fear is warning you about real danger and when it's just making things seem worse than they are."

Shawn took a deep breath, letting his dad's words sink in. *Fear isn't always the enemy.* He wasn't in danger—he was just scared of what he couldn't see.

Taking another step forward, he called louder, "Oscar!"

Then, they heard it—a faint whimper.

Shawn's heart leaped. "That's him!"

He broke into a run, ignoring the branches that scratched his arms. His fear melted into urgency. He needed to reach Oscar.

The whimper came again, closer now. Shawn swung the flashlight toward the sound and gasped.

Oscar was trapped between a fallen log and a tangle of thorny vines. His golden fur was covered in dirt, and his eyes were wide and scared.

Shawn dropped to his knees. "It's okay, buddy. I'm here."

Dad helped him pull the vines away, careful not to hurt Oscar. As soon as he was free, the dog leaped into Shawn's arms, licking his face frantically. Tears burned in Shawn's eyes. "I was so scared I wouldn't find you."

Dad smiled. "But you did."

As they walked back, Oscar trotting beside them, Shawn realized something. He had walked into the woods, faced his fear, and emerged stronger. The darkness hadn't beaten him. His love for Oscar had been bigger than his fear.

What Shawn Learned

Shawn learned that fear isn't the enemy—it's a challenge. It can point toward the things that matter most. Facing his fear made him stronger; now, the dark didn't seem so scary anymore.

Affirmation for Facing Fear

Write this affirmation in your notebook and repeat it whenever fear feels overwhelming:

"I am stronger than my fears, and every step I take makes me braver and more confident."

Try This

- Create a 'Bravery List' of things you want to overcome. Start with something small and check off each challenge as you face it.
- When you feel fear creeping in, pause and ask yourself: Is this real danger or just uncertainty?
- Write down a time you faced something scary. How did it feel? What did you learn?

Shawn's story reminds us that fear is just a doorway to strength. What fear will you challenge today?

Chapter 8: Culver and the Speech Contest

Culver's palms were sweaty as he stared at the sign-up sheet taped to the classroom door. "Annual Public Speaking Contest," it read in bold letters. His teacher had encouraged him to participate, but the thought of standing in front of the entire school made his stomach twist into knots.

What if I forget my words? What if everyone laughs at me? What if I completely mess up?

Culver sighed and turned away. He wanted to be braver, but his fear was like an invisible wall blocking his path. As he walked down the hallway, he bumped into Ms. Reynolds, his English teacher.

"Culver, I saw you looking at the contest sign-up. Thinking about it?" she asked with a warm smile.

"I don't know," he admitted. "I'm not ready. I'll probably freeze up."

Ms. Reynolds knelt down to his level. "Have you ever thought about reframing the way you see fear?"

Culver frowned. "Reframing?"

She nodded. "Instead of thinking 'I'm not ready,' what if you said, 'I'm preparing and improving'? You've already taken the first step just by considering it."

Culver thought about that as he walked home. Maybe fear wasn't telling him to stop—it was telling him that this challenge was important.

That evening, Culver sat at his desk with a blank sheet of paper. He wrote down every fear racing through his mind.

I'll forget my words. I'll mess up and embarrass myself. People will judge me.

Then, he looked at each fear and wrote an alternate outcome.

I might forget a word, but I'll keep going. I might make mistakes, but I'll learn from them. Most people will respect me for trying, not judge me.

He read through his new list and felt something shift inside him. Maybe fear wasn't his enemy—it was a sign that he was stepping into something meaningful.

Determined to try, Culver started practicing in front of the mirror. He imagined the audience clapping, his voice clear and strong. Every night, he practiced a little more, picturing success instead of failure.

One evening, his dad noticed him rehearsing. "I'm proud of you for pushing yourself," he said. "Remember, it's not about being perfect. It's about growing."

Culver nodded. Maybe he wasn't perfect, but he was improving.

On the morning of the contest, Culver's nerves returned in full force. As he stepped onto the stage, his hands gripped the microphone, his heartbeat thundering in his ears. The auditorium was packed, and hundreds of eyes watched him, waiting.

He took a shaky breath. *I can do this.*

"I used to be afraid of speaking in front of people," he began, his voice unsteady. A few whispers rippled through the crowd, but he didn't let them distract him. He planted his feet firmly, lifted his chin, and continued. "But I realized something—fear isn't a stop sign. It's a challenge. And today, I chose to rise to it."

His voice strengthened, and each word flowed with more confidence. He spoke about his journey, the way fear had tried to hold him back, and how he had chosen to rewrite the story in his mind. The crowd leaned in, captivated. By the time he reached his final words, he could barely hear himself over the roaring applause.

Culver stepped back from the microphone, his heart still racing—but this time, not from fear. It was from triumph.

What Culver Learned

Culver learned that fear isn't an enemy—it's a teacher. By reframing his fear, focusing on success, and preparing himself, he turned anxiety into accomplishment.

Affirmation for Facing Challenges

Write this affirmation in your notebook and repeat it whenever fear feels overwhelming:

"I embrace challenges with courage, knowing that every step forward makes me wiser, stronger, and more prepared for success."

Try This

- Write down a fear and create an alternate ending where you succeed.
- Visualize yourself overcoming a challenge and feeling proud.
- Talk to someone who has overcome a similar fear and learn from their experience. Ask them what helped them the most.

Culver's story reminds us that fear is just a story waiting for a new ending. What fear will you rewrite today?

Part 4: Rising Strong: The Power of Resilience

Hey, Challenger!

Have you ever tried something and failed? Maybe you lost a big game, got a bad grade, or felt like giving up on something important. It happens to everyone. Even the most successful inventors have faced setbacks. But instead of giving up, they used their setbacks to push forward, learn, and improve.

Resilience means getting back up, no matter how many times you fall. Every setback is a chance to learn, grow, and come back even stronger.

In this section, you'll meet boys who faced tough challenges but refused to let failure define them. By the end, you'll have the tools to build resilience and turn obstacles into opportunities. Ready to rise stronger? Let's go!

Chapter 9: Lucian and the Skateboard

Lucian always wanted to be the coolest kid in class. He wasn't the fastest runner, the best artist, or the smartest student, but he knew how to make people laugh. He figured if he could impress his classmates with a jaw-dropping trick or the funniest joke, he'd finally be noticed.

One afternoon, while sitting in the cafeteria, he overheard his friends talking about a kid from another school who had pulled off a crazy skateboard trick that had gone viral online. Inspiration struck.

If I can pull off something just as cool, everyone will think I'm amazing! He thought.

That weekend, Lucian spent hours practicing a skateboard trick he had seen on TV—jumping off the bench and landing perfectly on his board. He imagined the cheers, the admiration, the way everyone would chant his name. By Monday morning, he was buzzing with excitement.

At lunchtime, Lucian stood up on the cafeteria bench, his skateboard in one hand, his heart pounding. "Hey, guys! Watch this!" he called out, making sure he had everyone's attention.

The cafeteria went silent. The anticipation in the air was thick. *This is it,* he thought. *My big moment.*

He took a deep breath, bent his knees, and leaped.

Everything happened in a blur. His skateboard shot out from under him, and instead of landing smoothly, his foot slipped. He flailed wildly, arms windmilling, before landing flat on his back. The impact sent his lunch tray flying, splattering mashed potatoes and juice all over his face.

For a moment, there was dead silence.

Then came the laughter.

Loud, booming, unstoppable laughter. It echoed in the cafeteria, bouncing off the walls and ringing in his ears. Someone snorted. Someone else pointed. A group of kids clapped mockingly.

Lucian's face burned. He wanted to disappear. *This wasn't how it was supposed to happen!*

The rest of the day was a blur. Whispers followed him down the hall. Kids reenacted his wipeout in exaggerated, dramatic motions. Even the usually kind janitor gave him a knowing smirk while mopping up the mess he had made.

Lucian skipped his afternoon class and hid in the library. He buried his face in his arms, wishing he could turn back time.

"This is the worst day ever," he mumbled to himself.

Just then, Ms. Bennett, the school librarian, sat beside him. "Tough day?" she asked kindly.

Lucian groaned. "I made a complete fool of myself."

Ms. Bennett smiled. "And what are you going to do about it?"

"What can I do?" he muttered. "I'll never live this down."

She thought for a moment before saying, "You know, resilience isn't about avoiding embarrassing moments. It's about how you handle them. You can either let this moment define you, or you can learn from it and move forward."

Lucian frowned. "How do I do that?"

Ms. Bennett pulled a book from the shelf and flipped it open to a page. "Start by reframing your story. Instead of thinking, 'I failed, and everyone hates me,' ask yourself, 'What can I do now that will make me stronger?'"

Lucian sighed. He wasn't sure he could just "move forward." But he didn't want to be the joke of the school forever, either.

The next morning, Lucian walked into class expecting more laughter. And yes, there were a few kids who smirked at him. But instead of slinking to his seat, he stood in front of the room.

"Alright, let's get it over with," he announced with a grin. "Who wants to hear about the *greatest* skateboard fail of all time?"

The class went silent.

Then someone chuckled. Then another. Soon, laughter filled the room—not the mocking kind, but the kind that came from amusement, from seeing someone brave enough to laugh at themselves.

Lucian exaggerated every detail—how he had soared through the air like an action hero, how time had slowed as he saw his mashed potatoes flying, how he had landed with "grace" worthy of a cartoon character.

By the end of the story, his classmates weren't laughing *at* him anymore—they were laughing *with* him.

Something shifted that day. Instead of being the kid who wiped out, Lucian became the kid who owned his moment, who didn't let embarrassment crush him.

But he didn't stop there. Instead of trying to impress his classmates with tricks, he started helping them with things he was actually good at—helping Sarah understand math, giving Tim advice on jokes, and helping Jason improve his skateboard stance.

Day by day, he built himself back up—not by proving how "cool" he was, but by being himself.

What Lucian Learned

Lucian learned that resilience isn't about avoiding failure—it's about what you do after. He discovered that mistakes don't define you—how you respond to them does. By embracing his mistake, reframing the experience, and focusing on helping others, he found real confidence, not just the illusion of it.

Affirmation for Resilience

Write this affirmation in your notebook and repeat it whenever things don't go as planned:

"Every challenge makes me stronger. I learn, I grow, and I rise again."

Try This

- Think about a time you made a mistake. How can you reframe it into a learning experience?
- Keep a resilience journal where you write about challenges you've overcome with determination.
- Identify a challenge you're currently facing and list three ways you can take positive action to overcome it.

Lucian's story reminds us that setbacks are just setups for comebacks. What will you rise from today?

Chapter 10: Zachary and the Question

Zachary sat in his chair, staring at the textbook before him. He could feel his palms sweating as his teacher, Mr. Carson, scanned the classroom, looking for someone to answer the next question.

“Zachary,” Mr. Carson called.

His heart dropped. He hadn’t been paying attention—again. His mind had wandered, lost in thoughts of basketball practice later that afternoon. Now, every pair of eyes in the room was on him. He swallowed hard.

“I… I don’t know,” he mumbled, his cheeks burning red.

A few students giggled. Someone whispered, “Classic Zachary.”

Mr. Carson didn’t look disappointed, just expectant. “That’s okay. Let’s try again tomorrow.”

But Zachary barely heard him. His embarrassment was too loud, drowning out everything else. He spent the rest of the class staring at his desk, wishing he could disappear.

That night, Zachary sat in his room, replaying the moment over and over in his mind. He hated feeling like that—small, unprepared, ashamed. He decided he was done with that. If Mr. Carson called on him again, he wanted to have an answer. So, for the first time in a long time, he opened his textbook and actually studied. He made flashcards, wrote notes, and even asked his older sister, Maria, to quiz him. At first, it was frustrating—he got things wrong more often than he got them right. But he remembered something his dad always told him: *Every mistake is a step toward improvement.*

Day by day, his confidence grew. He didn't just memorize facts—he started to understand the lessons.

A week later, Mr. Carson asked another question. Zachary hesitated, then, before he could stop himself, raised his hand.

"Yes, Zachary?"

The class turned to look at him. His stomach clenched, but he pushed through. "The answer is photosynthesis. It's how plants make their own food using sunlight."

Silence.

Then, Mr. Carson smiled. "Excellent explanation, Zachary."

A flicker of pride sparked in his chest. He had done it.

But as Zachary started answering more questions, a new problem emerged. Some students started whispering about him behind his back. "Teacher's pet," they murmured when he got an answer right. "Mr. Carson's favorite."

At first, the words stung. He had worked so hard, and now he was being teased for it. The old Zachary would have let that shut him down. But not this time.

Instead of letting their words get to him, he focused on what really mattered: learning. He realized that knowledge was its own reward.

And then he did something unexpected—he started helping others.

Zachary noticed that some of the same kids who teased him struggled with their own schoolwork. Instead of ignoring them, he offered to help. At first, they rolled their eyes. But slowly, they started accepting his help.

One day, Mark, the class monitor, came up to him after school. “Hey, uh, I don’t get this math homework. Can you help?”

Zachary grinned. “Sure.”

Before long, more students began asking for his help. The teasing stopped. He was no longer ‘the teacher’s pet’—he was the guy people could count on.

What Zachary Learned

Zachary learned that perseverance isn’t just about pushing through difficulties—it’s about believing in yourself, even when others doubt you. He turned his embarrassment into motivation and showed his classmates that success wasn’t about being perfect but about working hard and helping others.

Affirmation for Perseverance

Write this affirmation in your notebook and repeat it whenever you feel discouraged:

“Every challenge I face makes me wiser, stronger, and more determined. I am unstoppable in my journey of growth.”

Try This

- Think about a time you felt embarrassed or unprepared. How can you turn it into motivation?
- Set a small daily goal, like reading for 10 minutes or practicing a skill, and track your progress.
- Find someone struggling and offer to help—they might just become your greatest supporter.

Zachary's story reminds us that challenges aren't roadblocks—they're opportunities to grow. What will you persevere through today?

Chapter 11: Nigel and the Truth

Nigel clutched the broken remote control in his hands, his heart pounding in his chest. The smooth plastic was now cracked, the buttons barely holding on. He hadn't meant to break it—he had just been flipping it between his fingers when it slipped and hit the hard tile floor.

His mind raced. *What if Mom and Dad get mad? What if they think I'm careless?* He glanced at the bookshelf, then at the back of the couch. Without another thought, he shoved the remote deep under the cushions. *Maybe no one will notice.* But deep down, he knew that wasn't true.

At dinner that night, Nigel could barely focus on his plate. His dad picked up the TV remote to change the channel, but nothing happened. He pressed the buttons harder, frowning.

"What's wrong with this thing?" his dad muttered, shaking it.

Nigel felt his stomach twist. His little sister, Mia, giggled. "Maybe it's tired!"

His mom sighed. "We just got that remote. What happened to it?"

Nigel swallowed. His palms felt sweaty. "Uh... maybe it just stopped working?" he suggested, avoiding their eyes.

His dad sighed. "I'll look at it tomorrow. Let's just use the buttons on the TV for now."

Relief washed over Nigel. He had dodged a bullet. *But for how long?*

Over the next few days, Nigel could barely concentrate at school. He felt like the remote was following him everywhere, whispering, *You should have told the truth.*

By the time he got home, the guilt had twisted into something unbearable.

Then, it got worse.

His mom was cleaning the couch when she found the remote. "Nigel?" she called. "Did you know this was under here?"

His stomach clenched. "Uh... no?"

His mom narrowed her eyes. "It's cracked."

Silence.

The truth pressed against his lips, but he couldn't get it out. His dad walked in, noticing the look on Mom's face. "Nigel," he said calmly. "Is there something you want to tell us?"

Nigel's face burned. His heart pounded so loudly he could barely hear. He had two choices: continue the lie or finally own up to it.

Tears pricked at his eyes. "I… I broke it," he admitted in a whisper.

The words felt like bricks falling from his shoulders.

For a moment, no one said anything. Then his dad sighed. "Nigel, why didn't you tell us?"

"I was scared," he admitted. "I didn't want you to be mad."

His mom's face softened. "We're not mad that you broke the remote. Accidents happen. But hiding the truth? That's the problem."

Nigel looked down. "I know. I should have said something."

His dad nodded. "Being honest—even when it's hard—is how you grow."

Nigel wiped his eyes and took a deep breath. "I'm sorry. I won't hide things again."

That night, Nigel thought about what had happened. He realized that hiding things only made problems worse. Instead of feeling relieved, he had felt awful.

The next time he accidentally knocked over a glass of water, he immediately grabbed a towel and told his mom. "I spilled this, but I'll clean it up."

His mom smiled. "That's the right way to handle it."

Nigel felt something new—pride. He wasn't running from mistakes anymore. He was learning from them.

What Nigel Learned

Nigel learned that hiding mistakes doesn't make them go away. Owning up to them, even when it's scary, is what truly makes you strong. Mistakes are just lessons in disguise.

Affirmation for Honesty

Write this affirmation in your notebook and repeat it whenever you feel afraid to admit a mistake:

"I am brave enough to be honest. Every mistake is a chance to learn and grow."

Try This

- The next time you make a mistake, take a deep breath and own up to it immediately.
- Write about a time you were honest, even when it was hard. How did it feel afterward?

- Encourage a friend who's afraid to admit a mistake—sometimes, they just need support.

Nigel's story reminds us that honesty isn't just about telling the truth—it's about being strong enough to face it. What truth will you be brave enough to share today?

Part 5: The Strength of Kindness and Connection

Hey, Difference-Maker!

True strength isn't just about being the fastest, the smartest, or the strongest. It's also about how you treat others. Imagine a world where no one helped their friends, shared a kind word, or stood up for someone in need. It wouldn't be a very great place, would it?

Real leaders, from firefighters rescuing people to scientists working together to solve big problems, all have one thing in common: *compassion*. They understand that kindness isn't weakness—it's *power*. It builds trust, creates friendships, and makes the world better for everyone.

In this section, you'll meet boys who learned that empathy, connection, and small acts of kindness can change lives—including their own. By the end, you'll discover how true strength comes not just from what you achieve but from *how you lift others up along the way*. Ready to make a difference? Let's begin!

Chapter 12: Adrian and the Beach Mission

Adrian stood at the edge of the shore, his shoes sinking slightly into the damp sand. The once beautiful beach, where he and his friends had spent countless summer days, was now unrecognizable. Wrappers, broken bottles, and discarded decorations from the New Year's Eve celebration littered the ground. The sight made his stomach churn.

"This is awful," he whispered to himself.

He glanced around. Other people walked by, shaking their heads but doing nothing. Some even took pictures as if it were just another social media post to scroll past. Adrian's fingers curled into fists. He couldn't just stand there. The beach had given him so many good memories—now, it was his turn to give back.

Determined, Adrian ran home and grabbed a pair of gloves and a trash bag. He knew he couldn't clean the entire beach alone, but he could start. When he returned, he crouched down and picked up the first piece of trash—a crumpled soda can, half-buried in the sand.

One by one, he filled his bag. It was exhausting, and the sun blazed down on him, but every time he looked up at the mess still left, he felt even more determined.

Then, he heard laughter behind him. A group of kids around his age were pointing at him.

"Look at him, playing janitor," one sneered.

Adrian clenched his jaw. He wanted to snap back, to tell them that at least he was doing something. But instead, he took a deep breath and kept going.

His mother's words echoed in his mind: *Kindness is louder than mockery, but only if you keep at it.*

After a few minutes, a shadow fell over him. He looked up and saw his best friend, Lily, standing there with her hands on her hips.

"You're really doing this all by yourself?" she asked, her voice filled with surprise.

Adrian wiped the sweat from his forehead. "Someone has to."

Lily was quiet for a moment. Then, without another word, she pulled out her phone, snapped a picture of Adrian picking up trash, and posted it to their community page.

Within minutes, the comments started rolling in.

That beach needs help!

I'll bring trash bags!

Meet you there in an hour!

Adrian blinked. Was this really happening?

By the afternoon, people started arriving—families, classmates, even some of the kids who had mocked him earlier. One of them, Jason, shuffled up awkwardly, rubbing the back of his neck.

"Hey, um... can I help?" Jason asked hesitantly.

Adrian could have turned him away, but he knew that wouldn't help anyone. He simply handed Jason a pair of gloves. "Yeah. Grab a bag."

Together, they worked. People carried trash bags, kids ran around collecting small pieces, and even some adults started making calls to get volunteers and the local news involved.

The ripple effect had begun.

After hours of work, the beach looked transformed. The once scattered garbage was gone, replaced with clean sand and neatly placed recycling bins. The sight filled Adrian with pride.

The mayor arrived just as the last bag was tied up. "This was incredible," she said, shaking Adrian's hand. "You started something really special today."

Adrian smiled. He hadn't done it for recognition, but knowing he had made a difference filled his heart with something deeper than pride—purpose.

As the sun set over the now pristine shore, Adrian realized something: empathy wasn't just about feeling bad for someone or something. It was about action. It was about seeing a problem and stepping up.

And that, he knew, was what truly made a difference.

What Adrian Learned

Adrian learned that empathy isn't just about understanding someone else's pain—it's about taking action to help. His kindness inspired others, proving that even small acts can create big change.

Affirmation for Empathy

Write this affirmation in your notebook and repeat it whenever you want to make a difference:

"I am capable of creating positive change, and my kindness can inspire others."

Try This

- Think of a place in your community that needs help and take one small action to improve it.
- Practice active listening today—let someone talk without interrupting or offering advice.
- Share a story of kindness with someone and ask them to pass it forward.

Adrian's story reminds us that empathy is more than just a feeling—it's an action. What will you do today to make the world a better place?

Chapter 13: Joshua and His New Friend

Joshua sat on the edge of the lunch table, picking at the sandwich his mom had packed for him. The cafeteria buzzed with chatter and laughter, but he felt disconnected as if the noise were a world away. He had friends—good ones—but something felt off today.

Then, he noticed someone new.

At the far end of the cafeteria, a boy sat alone, hunched over a book, barely touching his food. He looked nervous, constantly adjusting his glasses and darting glances around the room. His oversized sweater swallowed him, making him look even smaller. Joshua had never seen him before.

"Who's that?" Joshua asked his best friend, Malik.

Malik barely looked up from his tray. "No idea. New kid, I think. Looks kinda nerdy."

Joshua frowned. He knew what it felt like to be the odd one out. Just last year, he had switched schools, and it had taken him weeks to find his place. His stomach clenched at the memory of eating alone, pretending he didn't care.

He pushed his tray aside and stood up.

"Where are you going?" Malik asked, raising an eyebrow.

"To say hi."

Joshua walked over, feeling strangely nervous himself. What if the kid didn't want company? What if he thought Joshua was just another person here to make fun of him?

"Hey," Joshua said, sliding onto the bench across from him. "I'm Joshua."

The boy looked up, surprised. He blinked behind his thick glasses. "Oh. Um. Hi. I'm Evan."

Joshua glanced at the book in his hands. "You like sci-fi?"

Evan's eyes lit up. "Yeah! This one's about a scientist who builds a time machine but accidentally traps himself in another dimension."

Joshua grinned. "That sounds awesome. I love adventure books."

Evan hesitated, then smiled—a small, cautious smile, but a real one. "Really?"

Joshua nodded. "Yeah. And if you like sci-fi, you must check out *The Galaxy* series. It's got spaceships, time travel, and the best plot twists."

For the first time that day, Evan relaxed.

Over the next few days, Joshua kept sitting with Evan, and slowly, the new kid came out of his shell. He wasn't just quiet—he was incredibly smart, funny in a dry way, and full of random facts about space and history.

But not everyone was welcoming.

One afternoon, as they walked to class, Malik pulled Joshua aside. "Dude, why are you always hanging out with Evan?"

Joshua shrugged. "He's cool."

"He's weird."

Joshua narrowed his eyes. "So what?"

Malik sighed. "People are talking. You don't want to get labeled a nerd too, do you?"

Joshua's stomach twisted. A few months ago, he might have cared. But now, looking at Evan—who had finally started smiling more, who actually looked forward to the lunchtime instead of dreading it—Joshua knew there was only one right answer.

"I don't care," he said firmly. "Evan's my friend."

Malik rolled his eyes and walked away.

Joshua took a deep breath. It stung, losing Malik's approval. But deep down, he knew he had made the right choice.

As the weeks passed, Evan became a real part of their school community. He joined the science club and even started helping Joshua with math, something Joshua had always struggled with.

One day, after school, Evan turned to Joshua and said, "You know, I was really scared to come here."

Joshua frowned. "Why?"

Evan adjusted his glasses. "I've always been the weird, nerdy kid. I figured no one would want to be my friend."

Joshua grinned. "Well, turns out you were wrong."

Evan laughed, and Joshua felt a warmth spread through him. Friendship wasn't about fitting in—it was about finding people who made you feel like you belonged.

And Evan belonged.

What Joshua Learned

Joshua learned that real friendship isn't about popularity—it's about connection. By stepping out of his comfort zone and standing by Evan, he found a friendship that made them both stronger.

Affirmation for Building Community

Write this affirmation in your notebook and repeat it when you need the courage to connect with others:

"I am open to new friendships, and I welcome others with kindness and understanding."

Try This

- Look for someone who might be feeling left out and start a conversation with them.
- Join a group or club that aligns with your interests and make new friends.
- Stand up for someone when others exclude them—kindness is more powerful than peer pressure.

Joshua's story reminds us that true strength lies in bringing people together. Who will you welcome into your world today?

Part 6: Dream Big, Take Actions

Hey, Visionary!

What would you do if fear didn't hold you back? Would you invent something groundbreaking, start your own business, or explore the deepest parts of the ocean? The biggest difference between those who achieve their dreams and those who don't isn't talent—it's the *courage to take action.*

But dreaming big doesn't mean waiting for the perfect moment. It means starting *now*—even if it's just a tiny step. Every great achievement begins with someone who dares to believe in themselves and takes that first bold move.

In this section, you'll read about boys who refused to let fear or obstacles stand in their way. They set their sights high, took risks, and proved that anything is possible with determination and action. By the end, you'll have the mindset and tools to do the same.

So, what's the dream that excites you? What bold step will you take next? Let's make it happen!

Chapter 14: Alexander and the Code

Alexander had always been fascinated by how things worked. From the way stars twinkled in the night sky to the mechanics behind his favorite video games, he wanted to understand it all. Science had always been his greatest passion. He spent hours watching documentaries, conducting small experiments at home, and flipping through pages of thick science textbooks. Yet, there was one problem—his classmates didn't share the same enthusiasm.

"Science is so hard," his best friend Jordan complained one afternoon. "I can never remember all those facts."

Alexander frowned. He had heard the same thing from many of his classmates. It wasn't that they didn't care about science—it was just that memorizing facts and formulas seemed impossible to them. That night, as he lay in bed staring at the glow-in-the-dark planets on his ceiling, an idea formed in his mind.

What if there was a way to make science fun and easy to remember?

The next morning, Alexander couldn't stop thinking about his idea. He knew coding was powerful—his older brother, Marcus, was a programmer, and Alexander had dabbled in a few coding lessons before. But this would be different. He wanted to build something that made learning science exciting.

He raced to his laptop and started sketching ideas. What if he created an app that turned science into a game? What if students could learn through interactive challenges instead of dull textbook reading?

But just as quickly as excitement filled him, doubt crept in.

I'm just a kid. Can I really do this?

Determined to try, Alexander asked Marcus for help. "Do you think I can build a coding app that helps people learn science?" he asked hesitantly.

Marcus raised an eyebrow. "That's a big dream," he said. "But if you work hard and stay persistent, I believe you can do it."

With that encouragement, Alexander got to work. He spent weeks watching coding tutorials, writing lines of code, and testing different ideas. But coding wasn't easy. Sometimes, he spent hours trying to fix a single bug. Other times, he wanted to quit.

One afternoon, after spending an entire day fixing a glitch that kept making the game crash, he groaned in frustration. "This is impossible!"

But then he remembered something his science teacher had said: *Even the greatest scientists faced failure before they found success.*

Taking a deep breath, he tried again. And again. Until finally, his code worked. His app was starting to come to life.

When Alexander shared his idea with his classmates, not everyone was supportive.

"You? Build an app?" one kid laughed. "That's impossible."

"Even if you make it, no one's going to use it," another added.

For a moment, their words stung. But then he thought about why he started this in the first place. He wasn't doing it for approval—he was doing it to help people. So, instead of letting their words discourage him, he kept going.

Finally, after months of work, Alexander's app was ready for testing. He nervously presented it to his science teacher, Ms. Robinson. She was quiet as she clicked through the game, trying the different challenges.

Then, she smiled. "Alexander, this is incredible."

She introduced the app to the class, and to his amazement, his classmates *loved it*. The game made learning fun, turning science facts into memory challenges and puzzles. Even the kids who had once doubted him were playing.

Word spread quickly. Soon, other teachers wanted to use the app in their classrooms. A local newspaper wrote an article about him. Before he knew it, Alexander was invited to present his app at a science fair.

Standing on the stage, looking out at the crowd, he felt a surge of pride. The boy who had once doubted himself had built something that was making a difference. And he knew this was just the beginning.

What Alexander Learned

Alexander learned that big dreams come with big challenges, but persistence and belief in yourself can turn them into reality. He realized that even when people doubt you, your determination can prove them wrong.

Affirmation for Big Dreams

Write this affirmation in your notebook and repeat it whenever you feel discouraged:

"I am capable of achieving my dreams, and I have the power to create something amazing."

Try This

- Think of a big dream you have and write down the first small step you can take toward it.
- Create a 'Dream Map'—a visual board or list of your goals and steps to achieve them. Add images, quotes, and reminders to keep you motivated.
- Challenge yourself to act today. No matter how small, do something that moves you closer to your dream—whether it's learning a skill, planning, or reaching out for advice.

Alexander's story reminds us that big dreams start with a single step. What will you build, create, or achieve today?

Chapter 15: Asher and His Journey with Colors

Asher sat in the corner of the art room, his brush gliding smoothly over the canvas. The strokes of blue and orange mixed perfectly, forming the beginnings of a breathtaking sunset. He had always loved painting—ever since he was little when he would watch his grandmother create stunning landscapes with just a few brushstrokes. But now, at his age, it wasn't so easy to just love painting.

Especially when the other boys laughed at him for it.

"Hey, Asher, still playing with colors?" Kyle, the school's basketball star, smirked as he walked past. His friends chuckled along with him.

Asher gripped his brush tighter, pretending he didn't hear them. It wasn't the first time they had teased him. While most of the boys in his class spent their free time dribbling basketballs and talking about sports, he spent his afternoons mixing colors and practicing his technique. He knew he was different, but did that mean he was wrong?

That night, as he stared at his unfinished painting, doubt crept into his mind. *Maybe I should try basketball. Perhaps I should stop painting. Maybe then they'd stop making fun of me.*

But deep inside, another voice whispered, *This is who you are. Don't give up just because they don't understand.*

The next morning, Asher made a decision. He would take his love for painting and turn it into something bigger. If the other boys thought painting wasn't "tough enough," he would show them how wrong they were.

He set a goal to complete three paintings by the end of the month and display them at the school's upcoming talent showcase. He broke it down into smaller steps: sketching the ideas, painting layer by layer, and ensuring each detail was perfect.

At first, it felt overwhelming. He had never worked on a deadline before, and every little mistake made him want to start over. But he reminded himself: *progress, not perfection.* He wasn't just painting anymore—he was proving to himself that he was capable of turning his dream into reality.

Word got around that Asher was planning to present his paintings at the showcase. Some people were supportive—his art teacher, Ms. Rina, beamed with pride when she heard. His little sister, Lisa, kept sneaking into his room to admire his work.

But the teasing from some of the other boys didn't stop.

"Why don't you do something real, Asher?" one of them snickered in the cafeteria. "Like sports?"

Asher clenched his fists. He wanted to shout that painting *was* real, that it required patience, skill, and vision. But instead, he took a deep breath. He didn't need to prove anything to them—he just needed to prove it to himself.

Each time doubt crept in, he reminded himself of his goal. He visualized the moment he would stand in front of his paintings at the showcase, proud of his accomplishments. He repeated his affirmations: *I am brave. I am capable. I am ready.*

The night of the showcase arrived. The school gallery was filled with people—students, parents, teachers. Asher's heart pounded as he set up his paintings on the display boards.

As the event began, students showed off their talents—singing, playing instruments, performing dance routines. Then, it was Asher's turn. He stood beside his paintings, waiting.

Some of the boys from his class walked by smirking. "Nice drawings," one muttered.

Asher straightened his shoulders. "They're paintings," he corrected, his voice steady. "And I worked really hard on them."

Then something unexpected happened. A woman, an art teacher from a nearby high school, stopped to admire his work. "These are incredible," she said, her eyes full of admiration. "You have real talent."

Slowly, more people gathered around. His classmates who had never paid attention before now looked at his paintings with wide eyes. His teacher snapped photos, and his parents beamed with pride.

Even Kyle, the basketball star, walked up and muttered, "I mean... they're pretty cool."

Asher smiled. He had done it. He had turned his passion into something real, something that demanded respect. He had proved to himself that following his dream was worth it.

What Asher Learned

Asher learned that dreams become a reality when you take action, even in the face of doubt and mockery. He discovered that bravery isn't just about doing what's expected—it's about standing strong in what makes you unique.

Affirmation for Courage

Write this affirmation in your notebook and repeat it whenever you feel discouraged:

"I am bold enough to step up when needed, resilient enough to learn from setbacks, and determined to achieve my goals."

Try This

- Set a daring challenge for yourself related to your passion and take the first step toward accomplishing it today.
- Find a mentor or role model who shares your dream and learn from their journey—ask for advice or study their work.
- Share your passion with someone new, even if it feels scary—your confidence might just inspire them, too.

Asher's story reminds us that staying true to yourself is the greatest strength of all. What dream will you turn into a reality today?

Chapter 16: Liam and the History Quiz

Liam had never thought of himself as bold. He was the kind of person who preferred to sit at the back of the class, listening rather than speaking. He admired people who could confidently raise their hands and answer questions, but he had never imagined himself as one of them. That changed the day Hudson, his best friend and the smartest kid in history class, got sick.

Hudson had been preparing for weeks to represent their school in the regional history quiz. He was their best chance at winning. But on the morning of the competition, Hudson's mom called the school—he had a fever and couldn't make it.

"Liam," their teacher, Mr. Porter, said, his expression serious. "You're Hudson's backup. You need to step in."

Liam's heart plummeted to his stomach. "Me?"

"Yes," Mr. Porter nodded. "You've been studying alongside Hudson. You can do this."

But Liam wasn't so sure. Hudson had been the one answering the tough questions during practice. Liam had just been there, listening and supporting him. But now, the entire team depended on him.

"I… I don't think I can," Liam mumbled, his palms sweaty.

"You won't know unless you try," Mr. Porter said gently.

Liam swallowed hard. He didn't feel courageous, but maybe it wasn't about feeling ready. Perhaps it was about stepping up when it mattered.

Sitting under the bright lights of the competition hall, Liam felt like he was about to faint. The questions came fast, and though he tried his best, doubt clouded his mind. He second-guessed himself, hesitated too long, and missed chances to score points. By the end of the quiz, their team had lost.

The disappointment was crushing. His teammates tried to be kind, saying they were proud he had stepped in at the last minute. But Liam couldn't shake the feeling that he had let everyone down—especially Hudson.

When he told Hudson what had happened, his friend just smiled. "So? We'll try again next year."

Liam blinked. "But I failed."

"You didn't fail. You just weren't ready *yet*," Hudson said. "Next year, we prepare together."

And just like that, Liam had a new goal. He wasn't going to let one failure define him.

The next day, Liam started studying—not because someone asked him to, but because he wanted to. He created a study plan, quizzed himself on flashcards, and even joined the history club. Hudson coached him, and slowly, the self-doubt started to fade.

At first, it was small. He started answering questions in class—not always right, but he spoke up. Then, he volunteered to help lead a history project. Each small step built his confidence. By the time the next quiz season arrived, he was ready. Standing on stage for the second time, Liam felt different. He wasn't shaking. He wasn't doubting himself. The questions came, and this time, he answered with certainty. Hudson sat beside him, giving him a reassuring nod every time he buzzed in.

By the end of the quiz, their school had won. The moment the announcer called their names, Liam felt genuinely happy. This wasn't just about winning—it was about proving to himself that he could be courageous.

What Liam Learned

Liam discovered that courage isn't about never feeling afraid—it's about continuing to move forward even when fear is present. He realized that setbacks are just stepping stones, and with determination and effort, any challenge can turn into a victory.

Affirmation for Never Giving Up

Write this affirmation in your notebook and repeat it whenever you feel uncertain:

"Every challenge I face is an opportunity to grow. I have the courage to keep going, no matter what."

Try This

- Take on the 'I Will Try' Challenge—pick one thing outside your comfort zone and give it your best shot this week.
- Start a 'Courage Journal' where you document moments of bravery, big or small, and reflect on how they made you feel.

- Partner with a friend and take on a challenge together—whether it's speaking up in class, trying a new skill, or entering a competition.

Liam's story reminds us that setbacks don't define us—our courageous actions do. What courageous step will you take today?

Part 7: The Power of Gratitude

Hey, Game-Changer!

Have you ever noticed how some people always seem happy, no matter what? It's not because their lives are perfect—it's because they've learned the secret to happiness: *gratitude*.

Gratitude isn't just saying "thank you." It's a way of seeing the world. It helps you focus on what you *do* have instead of what you don't. It makes challenges feel smaller, friendships feel stronger, and even ordinary moments feel special. The best part? The more you practice gratitude, the more confident, positive, and resilient you become.

In this section, you'll read about boys who discovered how gratitude transformed their outlook on life. By the end, you'll have your own way of using gratitude as a tool for happiness, success, and strength.

So, what's something you're grateful for today? Let's explore how gratitude can change everything!

Chapter 17: Ian and the Thank-You Note

Ian's stomach growled loudly as he sat in the cafeteria, staring at the empty space in front of him where his lunch should have been. He had been in such a hurry that morning, rushing out the door, that he had completely forgotten his lunch on the kitchen counter. Now, as his classmates unwrapped their sandwiches and opened their lunchboxes, he felt a wave of embarrassment crash over him.

"Forgot your lunch?" Elijah, one of the kids from his class, asked. Ian nodded, trying to act like it wasn't a big deal, but inside, he felt sad. What kind of kid forgets something as important as lunch? He slumped in his seat, already dreading the long, hungry afternoon ahead.

Just then, his friend Josh slid his sandwich across the table. "Here. Take half."

Ian blinked. "Are you serious?"

"Of course," Josh said with a shrug. "I'm not that hungry anyway."

Ian hesitated. He didn't want to take food from his friend, but his stomach protested again, deciding for him. "Thanks, Josh," he said softly, taking the half-sandwich. As he bit into it, he realized how much this small act of kindness meant to him.

The rest of the day, Ian couldn't stop thinking about what Josh had done. It wasn't just about the sandwich—it was the fact that Josh had offered it so easily, without making Ian feel bad or expecting anything in return. Ian had always heard people talk about gratitude, but he had never really thought about what it meant until now.

That night, as he lay in bed, he reflected on all the little things he often took for granted—a warm house, a caring family, and good friends like Josh. He realized that he had so much to be thankful for, even on days that didn't go perfectly.

The next morning, Ian made a decision. He would start paying more attention to the good things in his life, no matter how small. He grabbed an old notebook from his shelf and wrote at the top of the page: *Things I'm Grateful For.* Then, he added his first entry:

1. Josh shared his sandwich with me when I forgot my lunch.

It felt good to write it down like he was capturing a moment that mattered. He decided to add something new every day.

The next time Ian saw Josh, he handed him a small note. "What's this?" Josh asked, opening the note.

"It's just... a thank-you note," Ian said, feeling a little shy. "For yesterday."

Josh grinned. "Dude, you didn't have to do this."

"I know," Ian said, smiling. "But I wanted to."

Josh tucked the note into his backpack. "That's actually really cool. No one's ever given me a thank-you note before."

Ian felt sweet. Gratitude wasn't just about feeling thankful—it was about showing it.

Inspired by how good it felt to appreciate others, Ian kept going. He started noticing the little things more. He thanked his mom for making breakfast, complimented his teacher on an interesting lesson, and told his dad he appreciated their weekend soccer games. Each time, he saw how much it meant to the other person.

One day, he got an idea. "What if we started a gratitude board at school?" he asked Josh.

"A what?"

"A board where people can write things they're thankful for. Like, small things that make their day better."

Josh thought for a moment. "That's actually a great idea."

With their teacher's permission, they set up a giant poster near the cafeteria. At first, only a few students added things:

- "My mom packed my favorite lunch today."
- "I got an A on my test!"
- "Daniel helped me with my homework."

Soon, however, more and more students started contributing. The board filled up with messages of appreciation, and the energy in the school started to change. Instead of complaining about homework or tests, students started talking about the good things happening around them.

One day, their principal even stopped by. "This is an incredible idea," she said, reading the messages. "You boys have started something really special."

Ian beamed. He never expected that one small act—one shared sandwich—would lead to something this big. But that was the power of gratitude. One small moment could create ripples of kindness everywhere.

What Ian Learned

Ian learned that gratitude isn't just about saying "thank you"—it's about recognizing and appreciating the good things in life, no matter how small. He realized that even small acts of kindness can make a huge impact and that sharing gratitude makes the world a better place.

Affirmation for Gratitude

Write this affirmation in your notebook and repeat it daily:

"I choose to see and appreciate the good in my life, and I share my gratitude with others."

Try This

- Start a gratitude journal and write down three things you're thankful for each day.
- Write a thank-you note to someone who has helped or supported you and give it to them.
- Begin a gratitude challenge at school or home—encourage others to share what they appreciate.

Ian's story reminds us that gratitude can turn an ordinary moment into something extraordinary. What will you be grateful for today?

Chapter 18: Archie Finds Appreciation

Archie had never given much thought to the little things—running through the park, feeling the wind rush past his face, or even laughing so hard he could barely breathe. These were just everyday moments, things he had always done without thinking. Until one day, everything changed.

It started with a tickle in his throat, then a stuffy nose, then an awful heaviness in his head. By the next morning, he was wrapped in blankets, shivering and coughing, while his mom pressed a hand to his forehead and sighed. "You've got the flu, sweetheart. No school, no playing outside—just rest."

Archie groaned. Missing school was one thing, but being trapped indoors, unable to run and play, felt like a punishment. "But I was supposed to play soccer with Finn today," he mumbled.

His mom kissed his forehead. "Finn will still be there when you're better. Right now, you need to focus on resting."

Archie didn't have the energy to argue. On the first day, he mostly slept. The second day, he stared at the ceiling, bored beyond belief. By the third day, frustration settled deep in his chest. He missed fresh air. He missed moving. He missed being *himself.*

By day four, Archie felt a little better. He could sit up, and his fever had gone down, but he was still weak. His mom set a bowl of soup in front of him and sat beside him. "You've been pretty grumpy the past few days," she said gently. "Want to talk about it?"

Archie frowned at his soup. "I just hate being stuck inside. I never realized how much I loved running around until I couldn't do it."

His mom smiled. "You know, that's a kind of gratitude."

Archie blinked. "Gratitude?"

She nodded. "Sometimes, we don't appreciate things until they're taken away. But now, you *see* how special it is to run and play. And when you get better, you'll enjoy it even more."

That idea stuck with him. Maybe his mom was right. Maybe he had been so used to *having* everything—his energy, his health, his ability to run around—that he had never really appreciated it.

The next day, Archie felt strong enough to stand in front of his notice board—the one where he usually pinned up pictures of his favorite moments. Instead of just looking at old memories, he decided to add something new. He grabbed a marker and a sticky note, writing at the top: *Things I Appreciate.* Then, he thought about the past week and wrote his first notes:

1. Breathing freely without feeling like a weight is pressing on my chest.
2. I can see trees and sunshine through my window.
3. Mom making me soup and taking care of me.

He stepped back and looked at the notes pinned to the board. Even though he had been miserable, there had still been good things in his life, and now he could see them every day.

He decided he would keep adding new appreciation notes to the board every day, creating a wall of positivity he could look at whenever he needed a reminder.

By the time he was finally allowed outside, Archie felt like he had been released from a cage. The moment his feet hit the grass, he took off running, his heart pounding with excitement. He ran across the yard, then back again, breathing in the fresh air like it was the best thing in the world.

"Feeling better?" his dad called from the porch.

Archie grinned. "Way better!"

As he ran, he thought about all the little things he had never noticed before—the way the sky looked extra blue, the way the wind tickled his skin, the way his legs felt *alive* with movement. He had taken these moments for granted before, but not anymore.

That evening, he added more to his board:

4. Running without feeling weak.
5. The smell of fresh grass.
6. The sound of laughter when Finn tackled me during soccer.

Archie didn't just stop at his gratitude board. One day at school, he noticed his friend Olivia looking upset. "What's wrong?" he asked.

"I lost my favorite pencil," she mumbled.

Archie thought for a moment, then pulled a cool-looking pen from his backpack. "Here, you can have this one. I like it, but I think you need it more."

Her face lit up. "Really? Thanks, Archie!"

It felt *good* to share something, to make someone else smile. Maybe appreciation wasn't just about noticing good things—it was about *creating* them too.

That night, he had a new idea. "Mom, can we start an appreciation jar?"

She raised an eyebrow. "A what?"

"A jar in which we write down what we appreciate the most each day and place it inside. Then, we can read everything at the end of the month."

His mom smiled. "That's a great idea, Archie."

Together, they decorated an old jar, and Archie placed the first note inside: *I'm happy that I can run again.*

What Archie Learned

Archie learned that appreciation is a form of gratitude that isn't just about feeling thankful—it's about noticing the small joys in life, even when things aren't perfect. He realized that being sick had given him a gift: the ability to truly appreciate his health, his friends, and the little things that made each day special.

Affirmation for Appreciation

Write this affirmation in your notebook and repeat it daily:

"I embrace each day with gratitude and appreciation, knowing that even the smallest moments hold great value."

Try This

- Turn a section of your wall or a board into an 'Appreciation Space' where you pin pictures, notes, or small objects that remind you of happy moments.
- Start a 'My Moments' challenge—every day, take a picture or draw something that made you smile and add it to your gratitude space.
- Perform a random act of kindness to show gratitude for the people in your life.

Archie's story reminds us that gratitude is everywhere—we just have to take the time to see it. What are you grateful for today?

Part 8: Celebrating Your Inner Superhero

Hey, Trailblazer!

You don't need a cape or superpowers to be a hero. True heroes aren't just found in stories—they are real people who show courage, kindness, and strength every single day. And guess what? *You* have an inner hero, too, just waiting to be recognized and celebrated.

Being a hero isn't about being perfect. It's about knowing your strengths, believing in yourself, and standing up for what matters. It's about embracing who you are and using your confidence and courage to make a difference—whether that's helping a friend, chasing a big dream, or inspiring others through your actions.

In this section, you'll meet boys who discovered their own heroic qualities, proving that strength comes in many forms. By the end, you'll see that *you* have everything it takes to be your own hero—starting today.

So, what makes *you* a hero? Let's celebrate it!

Chapter 19: Jacob and His Architectural Plans

Jacob had always been fascinated by buildings. From towering skyscrapers to ancient ruins, every structure told a story, and he dreamed of creating something just as meaningful. As a child, he spent hours sketching castles, bridges, and futuristic cities, imagining the day he could turn his drawings into reality. But deep inside, fear held him back. He doubted if he could ever become a great architect like his grandfather.

His first attempt at building a model structure was an absolute disaster. He spent weeks designing a miniature replica of an old cathedral, carefully measuring every piece. But when he put the final piece in place, the structure collapsed into a heap of broken pieces. Frustrated and embarrassed, he wanted to quit. Maybe he wasn't meant to be an architect after all.

Jacob's art teacher, Mrs. Dawson, noticed his disappointment. "Every great architect has faced failure," she said, handing him a book filled with famous blueprints. "The key isn't in avoiding mistakes, but in learning from them."

With renewed determination, Jacob studied the blueprints closely, trying to understand what made them stable. He realized he had overlooked the foundation, the most crucial part of any structure. Inspired, he decided to try again.

To truly understand architecture, Jacob knew he had to see it up close. His grandfather took him to visit a famous skyscraper, but as they stepped onto the observation deck, Jacob's legs froze. The towering height made him dizzy.

His grandfather placed a reassuring hand on his shoulder. "Buildings stand tall because of strong foundations and fearless architects," he said. "You have the strength to overcome this fear."

Taking a deep breath, Jacob looked out at the skyline. Instead of fear, he saw possibility. He saw his future.

Back home, Jacob revisited his collapsed model. He reinforced the base, adjusted the balance, and studied architectural techniques. After several revisions, his new design stood firm. The moment he placed the final piece and saw it remain intact, a surge of pride filled him. He had turned his failure into a lesson.

His classmates and Mrs. Dawson admired his progress. "This is incredible work," she said. "Why don't you submit it to the Young Innovators' Contest?"

Jacob hesitated. Presenting his work to judges meant facing another fear—public speaking. But deep inside, he knew he had to take the next step.

The competition day arrived. As Jacob stood before the panel of judges, his hands trembled, and his mind threatened to go blank. But then, he remembered his journey—the failures, the late-night sketches, the moment he conquered his fear of heights.

He took a deep breath and spoke with passion, explaining how he had improved his design and why architecture mattered to him. His confidence grew with every word.

Though he didn't win first place, the judges were impressed. "You have a bright future in architecture," one of them told him. "Keep building."

Jacob continued challenging himself. He experimented with 3D modeling, explored different architectural styles with his grandfather, and even visited historical ruins with his parents to understand how ancient structures were built. Each experience deepened his love for architecture and strengthened his resolve. He recognized that regardless of the outcome, he had already begun moving toward his dreams—he had created a vision that could stand tall and strong.

What Jacob Learned

Jacob learned that failure isn't the end. He realized that his strengths—his creativity, determination, and willingness to learn—were what would truly make him a great architect. He discovered that fear dissipates when you take bold steps forward.

Affirmation for Strength

Write this affirmation in your notebook and repeat it whenever you face self-doubt:

"I am strong, capable, and ready to build my dreams, one step at a time."

Try This

- Create a list of your strengths and how they help you in your passions.
- Try something new that challenges your fears, just like Jacob faced his fear of heights.
- Build a small project—a model, a sketch, or a creative work—and reflect on what you learned in the process.

Jacob's story reminds us that dreams aren't built in a day, but with perseverance, every blueprint becomes a masterpiece. What will you build today?

Chapter 20: Mateo: The Little Forest Man

Mateo had always felt a deep connection to the earth. While other kids played video games or ran around the soccer field after school, he could be found in his backyard, his hands deep in the soil, carefully potting tiny saplings. He loved watching plants grow—each leaf unfolding, each root digging deeper into the earth, each flower blooming in its own time. His grandfather, an old farmer, often said, “A seed is a promise, Mateo. It holds all the possibilities of life.”

But not everyone saw it that way.

Mateo’s classmates often teased him. “Why do you spend all your time with dirt?” they would laugh. “You should be out playing sports, not playing with plants.”

At first, the teasing stung. He started keeping his passion to himself, growing plants only in the quiet of his backyard, away from prying eyes. But no matter how much he tried to ignore it, his heart still yearned for the green life he nurtured.

One day, while walking home from school, Mateo noticed something that made his heart ache. Behind his neighborhood was a small forest patch, once green and thriving, now dull and dying. The trees looked weak, the soil dry, and trash littered the ground. It had once been a place where birds chirped and children played, but now, it looked abandoned.

"Someone should do something," he muttered.

Then, he realized—he could be that someone.

With newfound determination, Mateo ran home and grabbed his gardening tools. That weekend, he went back to the patch, raking leaves, clearing litter, and loosening the dry soil. He planted small saplings, watered them, and whispered words of encouragement, just like his grandfather did when they planted vegetables together.

The first few days were lonely. The work was tiring, and at times, he wondered if he was making any difference at all. His hands were covered in blisters, and his clothes were stained with mud, but he refused to give up.

"Why are you wasting your time?" a boy from school sneered as he walked by.

Mateo clenched his fists, but instead of arguing, he took a deep breath. "Because I care," he said simply.

The boy rolled his eyes and walked away, but Mateo felt a surge of determination. He was no longer afraid of what others thought. He was doing what he loved, and that was all that mattered.

One afternoon, as Mateo watered the newly planted trees, he heard footsteps behind him. Turning around, he saw his neighbor, Sofia, watching curiously.

"Can I help?" she asked shyly.

Mateo's heart swelled with excitement. "Of course!" he grinned, handing her a small sapling.

Word spread, and soon, more kids from the neighborhood joined in. They brought their own tools, seeds, and ideas. Mateo showed them how to plant trees properly, how to care for them, and how to let nature breathe again. The once-forgotten forest patch was coming back to life.

The local community noticed, too. Parents, teachers, and even the mayor came to see what the children had done. They were amazed at how much had changed.

One day, an elderly woman patted Mateo on the shoulder and smiled. "You're our little forest man."

The name stuck, and soon, everyone in town knew about "The Little Forest Man."

Mateo's efforts didn't go unnoticed. A local newspaper wrote an article about the restored forest patch. Environmental groups reached out, offering support and more plants. Mateo was even invited to speak at his school about why nature mattered.

Standing on stage, Mateo felt his knees shake. Speaking in front of a crowd terrified him, but he remembered his grandfather's words: *A seed is a promise.*

He took a deep breath and spoke about his journey, about the importance of trees, and about how every small effort counts.

By the end of his speech, the entire auditorium clapped. Mateo realized something powerful—his love for plants wasn't just about him. It was about inspiring others to care, to take action, and to make the world greener.

That night, he sat in his backyard, looking up at the stars. He had once been afraid to let his light shine, but now, he knew he was exactly where he was meant to be.

And this was just the beginning.

What Mateo Learned

Mateo learned that true strength comes from embracing what makes you unique. He discovered that doing what you love can inspire others and that even small actions can make a big impact. Most importantly, he realized that when you let your light shine, you encourage others to do the same.

Affirmation for Shining

Write this affirmation in your notebook and repeat it whenever you need courage: **"I have faith in my passion, and I know that each small action I take makes a difference."**

Try This

- Think about something you love but have been afraid to share—take one small step toward embracing it today.
- Start a small project that reflects your passion, whether it's art, writing, music, or nature.
- Encourage a friend or family member to explore their own interests and shine in their own way.

Mateo's story reminds us that being yourself is the most powerful thing you can do. How will you let your light shine today?

Chapter 21: Sebastian and Water Polo

Sebastian had always felt out of place on the basketball court. His father, a former star player, had high hopes for him, believing that he would follow in his footsteps. But every time Sebastian dribbled the ball, passed it, or took a shot, something felt off. It wasn't that he didn't enjoy sports—he just didn't love basketball the way his father did.

What he truly loved was water polo.

Whenever he swam, he felt free. The water was where he belonged, where he felt strong, fast, and in control. Yet, he never had the courage to tell his father the truth. What if his dad was disappointed? What if his friends mocked him? Everyone expected him to be the next basketball star, but deep down, he knew that wasn't his dream.

One afternoon, after another frustrating basketball practice, Sebastian sat by the pool at school, watching the water polo team train. The players moved with agility and power, and their teamwork was fluid and dynamic. He could see himself out there, battling for the ball, feeling the rush of competition in the water.

"Why don't you join us?" Coach Rivera, the water polo coach, asked, noticing his interest.

Sebastian hesitated. "I… I don't know if I can. I told my dad I wanted to play basketball like him, but then I realized I didn't want to."

Coach Rivera nodded. "He will understand, Sebastian. It's about what you love. If this is what makes you happy, you owe it to yourself to try. Your dad will love you for that."

That night, Sebastian lay awake, his heart pounding. Could he really tell his father? Could he risk disappointing him?

Taking a deep breath, he decided it was time.

The next evening at dinner, Sebastian finally spoke up. "Dad, I need to tell you something."

His father looked up from his plate, curious. "What is it, son?"

Sebastian swallowed hard. "I don't want to play basketball anymore. I want to play water polo."

A heavy silence filled the room. His father's expression shifted from surprise to confusion. "Water polo? But you've been playing basketball for years. You have talent."

"I know," Sebastian said, his voice steady. "But I don't love it like you do. Every time I get in the water, I feel like I belong there. It's where I want to be."

His father exhaled, running a hand through his hair. "Are you sure about this?"

Sebastian nodded. "More than anything."

His father was quiet for a long moment. Then, finally, he nodded. "If this is what you truly want, I'll support you."

Relief flooded through Sebastian. He had expected anger and disappointment, but instead, he had been met with understanding.

With his father's blessing, Sebastian joined the water polo team. But the transition wasn't easy. Unlike basketball, where he had years of experience, water polo was a whole new challenge. He struggled with endurance, missed passes, and got outplayed by stronger teammates.

There were moments he doubted himself. Maybe he had made a mistake. Maybe he wasn't meant for this.

But every time he felt like giving up, he reminded himself why he was here. He stayed late after practice, swimming extra laps, practicing his shots, and learning from his teammates. Coach Rivera saw his dedication and pushed him even harder, helping him refine his skills.

One evening, his father came to watch practice. Sebastian noticed him standing by the bleachers, arms crossed. For a moment, nerves threatened to overtake him. But instead of freezing, he focused on what he had learned. He played his best game yet, scoring a crucial goal during the scrimmage.

Afterward, his father approached him. "You looked strong out there," he said. "I can see how much this means to you."

Sebastian smiled. "It does, Dad. It really does."

Months passed, and Sebastian's hard work paid off. He earned a spot on the starting lineup for the championship match. The pressure was intense, but this time, he wasn't afraid.

The game was fierce. The opposing team was tough, and the score remained close. With only a minute left on the clock, the ball came to Sebastian. His heart pounded, but he didn't hesitate. He took aim and fired a shot straight into the goal. The crowd erupted. His teammates cheered. And as the final whistle blew, his team had won the championship.

Sebastian's father rushed onto the pool deck, beaming with pride. "You did it, son," he said, clapping a hand on his shoulder. "I've never seen you so determined. So happy."

Sebastian grinned. "Because I finally did what I love."

What Sebastian Learned

Sebastian learned that being true to himself was more important than meeting others' expectations. He realized that fear fades when passion takes its place and that hard work and dedication make dreams a reality. Most of all, he learned that living authentically brings the greatest success of all—happiness.

Affirmation for Being True to Yourself

Write this affirmation in your notebook and repeat it whenever you need courage:

"I choose my own path, and I am proud of who I am."

Try This

- Imagine your life a year from now if you fully pursued your passion—write a short letter to your future self about how it feels to live authentically.
- Write down three values that are most important to you and think about how you can align your actions with them.
- Share your journey—whether through a conversation, a letter, or a small project that reflects your passion—to inspire others and show them that embracing what you love is worth it.

Sebastian's story reminds us that true success comes from following our passions. What bold step will you take today?

Bonus Chapter: David and the No-Phone Family Dinner Challenge

David loved family dinners. It was one of the few times everyone sat together at the table. His parents, his younger sister Emma, and sometimes even his grandparents would join. The kitchen smelled of delicious food, the table was filled with all their favorites, and the room was usually full of chatter and laughter. But tonight, something felt different.

As David sat down, he noticed his dad checking emails on his phone, his mom scrolling through messages, and Emma watching a video on her tablet. Even David had been texting his friends just moments ago.

At first, he didn't think much of it, but as they ate, he realized something—nobody was really talking. Instead of sharing stories or laughing together, everyone was looking at their screens.

That's when an idea popped into his head.

David cleared his throat and sat up straight. "Hey, guys!" he said loudly.

Nobody looked up.

He tried again. "HEY, GUYS!"

His mom blinked and put her phone down. "What is it, David?"

David hesitated for a second. Would they think his idea was silly? But then he remembered what his teacher once said: *If you want to change something, sometimes you have to be the first to act.*

"I have a challenge for all of us," he said. "Let's do a **No-Phone Challenge!** We put our phones away for the rest of dinner—no texting, no games, no emails. Just talking, laughing, and actually spending time together."

Emma groaned. "But I was watching something!"

His dad sighed. "I still have work emails to check."

Even his mom hesitated. "But what if something important comes up?"

David took a deep breath. "I think *this* is important," he said. "We're all here together, but we're not really here. Don't you miss the way dinners used to be? When we actually talked?"

For a moment, no one said anything. Then, his grandpa, who had been watching from the head of the table, nodded. "David's got a point. Back in my day, we didn't have phones at the dinner table, and somehow, we still had a great time."

His mom smiled. "You know what? He's right." She placed her phone face down on the counter. "I'm in."

Everyone else agreed, one by one. Some grumbled, but soon, all the phones were stacked in the middle of the table.

At first, things felt weird. Nobody was used to sitting without checking their phones.

But then, David's dad cleared his throat. "Alright, since we're actually paying attention to each other now, let's do something fun. Everyone goes around and shares their favorite family memory."

David grinned. This was what family dinners were supposed to be like.

His grandpa shared a story about a camping trip during which their tent got soaked in the rain. His dad laughed about the time Emma tried to bake cookies and almost set the kitchen on fire. His mom talked about how she and his dad used to go on picnics when they first met.

Then, something amazing happened.

Instead of feeling bored without their phones, everyone started talking more. Emma told a joke so funny that David nearly choked on his drink. His dad and grandpa started playfully arguing over who made the best pancakes. His mom and grandma talked about their favorite childhood games.

It felt like a real family dinner for the first time in a long time.

By the time the main course was served, nobody even thought about their phones.

David's dad looked at the stack of devices in the middle of the table and then at his son. "That was actually nice," he admitted. "Maybe we should do this more often."

Emma, who had been the most resistant, grinned. "Okay, fine. It wasn't *that* bad."

His mom nodded. "I think we just started a new tradition. From now on, at least once a week, we have a **No-Phone Family Dinner.**"

Everyone cheered in agreement.

David sat back in his chair, feeling proud. He had done something important. He had led his family toward something better.

And as they continued talking and laughing late into the evening, David realized something else—sometimes, the best way to inspire others is to *show* them what truly matters.

As they cleared the table, his grandpa patted him on the shoulder. “You know, David, tonight really felt like a true Thanksgiving.”

David smiled. He couldn’t agree more.

What David Learned

David learned that real leadership means taking action—even when it feels uncomfortable. He saw that small changes, like putting away phones for dinner, can make a huge difference. Most importantly, he realized that true connections aren’t made on screens; they’re made by being present with the people we love.

Affirmation for Meaningful Connections

Write this affirmation in your notebook and say it whenever you need to remind yourself to be present:

“I am grateful for the people in my life. Every moment I spend with them is a chance to create wonderful memories.”

Try This

- Plan your own No-Phone Challenge at home! Talk to your family about putting away all devices for a meal. See what fun things you can do together instead!
- Create a memory jar. Every time something fun happens, write it down and put it in a jar. At the end of the year, read them with your family!
- Ask a grandparent or older family member what their childhood dinners were like. What games did they play? What stories do they remember most?

David’s story reminds us that real moments matter more than screens. What will you do to be more present today?

The Journey Ahead

Hey, Champion!

Look how far you've come! Throughout this journey, you've explored courage, confidence, resilience, kindness, and gratitude—powerful tools that can help you face any challenge and chase any dream. But here's the best part: *this is just the beginning.*

Every great adventure continues with new choices, new challenges, and new opportunities to grow. The lessons you've learned don't end here—they'll guide you as you take bold steps, stand up for what's right, and become the best version of yourself.

Remember, you don't have to be perfect to be strong. You don't have to know everything to be confident. And you don't have to wait for someone else to lead—you already have everything inside you to be a hero in your own story.

No matter where life takes you, always believe in yourself, keep pushing forward, and never stop dreaming big.

With faith in your strength and endless belief in you…

Your Biggest Cheerleader

Sati

Thank You

Hey there, Amazing Champ!

You made it to the end—high five! I'm so proud of you for taking this journey with me. I hope you had fun, discovered new things, and feel even more ready to chase your dreams and take on the world!

Thank you from the bottom of my heart for reading this book. It means so much to me that you joined this adventure. But now, I need a small favor. Could you ask your grown-up to leave a review? It's quick and easy and helps me create more stories for you and other incredible kids. Just a little nudge (maybe a big "Please!") and let them know how much you enjoyed it.

Scan Me

>> Leave a Review on Amazon<<

Thank you for being so awesome—you're my superhero!

About the Author

Sati Siroda is an inspirational author passionate about empowering young minds through storytelling. With a knack for weaving simple yet profound tales, Sati inspires kids, teens, and young adults to embrace their unique potential and navigate life with courage and purpose.

Sati's diverse academic journey—from engineering to education, business, and communication—combined with her extensive travels and time spent in various countries for education, business, and skill development shapes her holistic storytelling approach. Her experience teaching in schools and universities has further enriched her understanding of young minds, helping her find her path as a storyteller who connects deeply with her audience. Her multifaceted background enables her to connect with readers in relatable and innovative ways. Her stories are fueled by a belief in the transformative power of narrative. Drawing from her expertise in strategic communication and her love for literature, Sati crafts engaging, uplifting books that instill resilience, emotional intelligence, and self-confidence in her readers. Her mission is clear: to inspire the next generation to dream fearlessly, think critically, and approach life's challenges with creativity and optimism.

Through her heartfelt stories, Sati creates a world where every page becomes a stepping stone toward growth, and every character serves as a guiding light. She warmly invites readers of all ages to embark on a journey of self-love, self-discovery, and empowerment through the enchantment of her books.

Stay connected with Sati Siroda on Instagram: *@SatiSiroda.*

www.ingramcontent.com/pod-product-compliance
Lightning Source LLC
Chambersburg PA
CBHW062143160726
48282CB00027B/929
* 9 7 8 8 1 9 8 5 3 3 7 2 2 *